Engineering Our World

How a Ship Is Built

By Sam Aloian

Gareth Stevens
PUBLISHING

Please visit our website, www.garethstevens.com. For a free color catalog of all our high-quality books, call toll free 1-800-542-2595 or fax 1-877-542-2596.

Library of Congress Cataloging-in-Publication Data

Aloian, Sam.
 How a ship is built / Sam Aloian.
     pages cm. — (Engineering our world)
 Includes index.
ISBN 978-1-4824-3915-1 (pbk.)
ISBN 978-1-4824-3916-8 (6 pack)
ISBN 978-1-4824-3917-5 (library binding)
1. Shipbuilding—Juvenile literature. I. Title.
VM150.A56 2016
623.82—dc23
                                    2015027113

First Edition

Published in 2016 by
Gareth Stevens Publishing
111 East 14th Street, Suite 349
New York, NY 10003

Copyright © 2016 Gareth Stevens Publishing

Designer: Samantha DeMartin
Editor: Ryan Nagelhout

Photo credits: Cover, p.1 Photobank gallery/Shutterstock.com; caption boxes stoon/Shutterstock.com; background Jason Winter/Shutterstock.com; p. 5 Nickolay Khoroshkov/Shutterstock.com; p. 7 karnoff/Shutterstock.com; p. 9 Hans Christiansson/Shutterstock.com; p. 11 (double hull) courtesy of The Canadian Association of Petroleum Producers; p. 11 (aircraft carrier) David Acosta Allely/Shutterstock.com; p. 11 (tanker) Lledo/Shutterstock.com; p. 11 (cruise ship) Ruth Peterkin/Shutterstock.com; p. 13 Khrushchev Georgy/Shutterstock.com; p. 15 Bogdan VASILESCU/Shutterstock.com; p. 17 jordache/Shutterstock.com; p. 19 ES3DStudios/Shutterstock.com; p. 20 (tape) Sean MacD/Shutterstock.com; p. 20 (straw) Rakic/Shutterstock.com; p. 20 (scissors) Vladvm/Shutterstock.com; p. 20 (crayon) WachiraS/Shutterstock.com; p. 21 (girl) Serhiy Kobyakov/Shutterstock.com.

Printed in the United States of America

CPSIA compliance information: Batch #CS16GS: For further information contact Gareth Stevens, New York, New York at 1-800-542-2595.

Contents

Words in the glossary appear in **bold** type the first time they are used in the text.

All Aboard!

Ships are an important means of travel. Cruise ships take people across oceans to sunny vacation spots. The military uses giant ships to keep us safe and move planes from place to place. Other ships move millions of things from place to place to be bought and sold.

These days, ships have grown larger and are full of **technology**, but how we make them is largely the same as it's been for many years. Let's put on our hard hats and take a look at how a ship is built!

Building Blocks

A boat is a much smaller form of a ship. Ships are very large and can safely travel over deeper waters.

There are many different kinds of ships, each with its own purpose on the water.

Floating First

All boats have a simple goal: to float! The ability to float in water is called buoyancy. When a boat is put in water it displaces, or takes the place of, an amount of water equal to its weight.

Boats float when they're less **dense** than the water they're in. The weight of the water, however, also puts **pressure** on the sides of a boat. That means builders have to use **materials** that are strong without being very dense.

Building Blocks

A crack or leak in the outer walls of a boat, called the hull, can cause it to sink.

Buoyancy pushes a boat up against the force of gravity, the force that pulls objects toward Earth's center.

gravity

density of boat

density of water

buoyancy

Wood on the Water

The first boats were made of wood, which often naturally floats and is light and strong. Pieces of wood were fitted together and made watertight to stop leaks that could sink the boat. Early boats often moved using sails to catch the wind. They also used paddles, which strong people rowed in the water to make the boat move.

By studying the science of how boats float and how they move in water, shipbuilders have been able to make ships bigger and faster today than these early wooden boats.

Building Blocks

People who **design** large ships are called naval architects.

Sailboats and rowboats were some of the earliest man-made floating objects, but today's ships are much larger.

Steel and Air

Shipbuilders have lots of tricks to design large ships that are buoyant despite using heavy materials. Large ships have a hull made of two pieces of metal filled with air. The steel hull is heavy and strong, but the air is much lighter than water, so the boat is buoyant.

Naval architects work to make sure ships won't capsize, or tip over. Flat-bottomed boats are more **stable** in water, while ships with pointed bottoms move through water more easily.

Building Blocks

Naval architects need to study how solid matter moves in **fluids** like water. The study of fluids in motion is called hydrokinetics. The study of fluids at rest is hydrostatics.

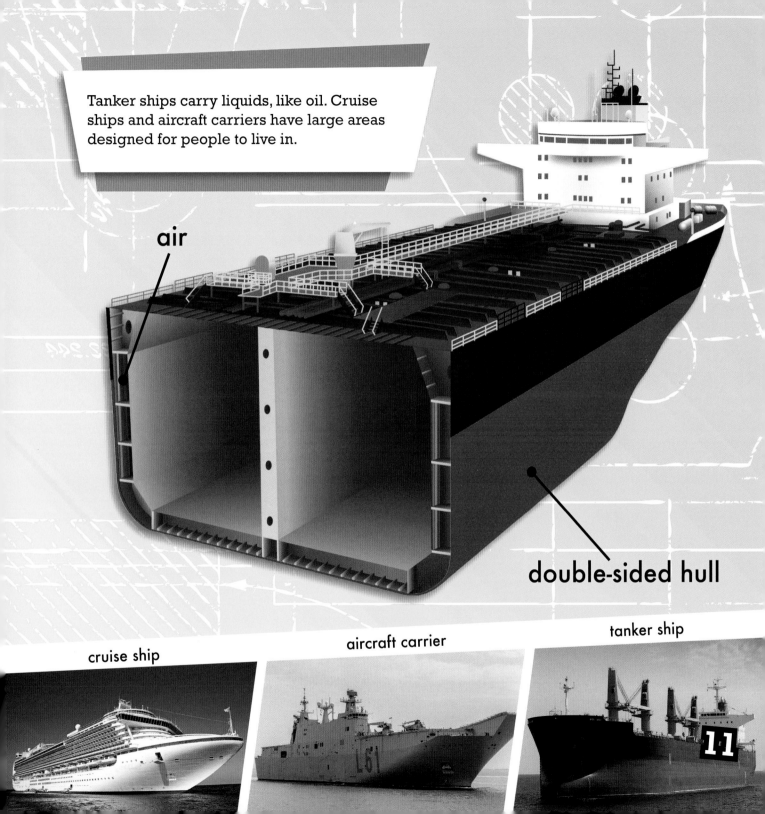

Tanker ships carry liquids, like oil. Cruise ships and aircraft carriers have large areas designed for people to live in.

air

double-sided hull

cruise ship

aircraft carrier

tanker ship

11

Start on Land

Once a naval architect has made designs for a ship, the shipbuilders must make sure they have all the materials and workers they need to build it. Ships are built at a shipyard. While shipyards are built near water, smaller ships start life on land. Larger ships are built at a **dry dock**.

The hull of a ship is built first. Large pieces of metal are put together and brought to the dry dock, then **welded** to form the hull. The main backbone of the ship's hull, called the keel, is built first.

Building Blocks

Tall **structures** called ways are spaced along the outside of a ship's hull to support it during construction. They're made of concrete and wooden blocks.

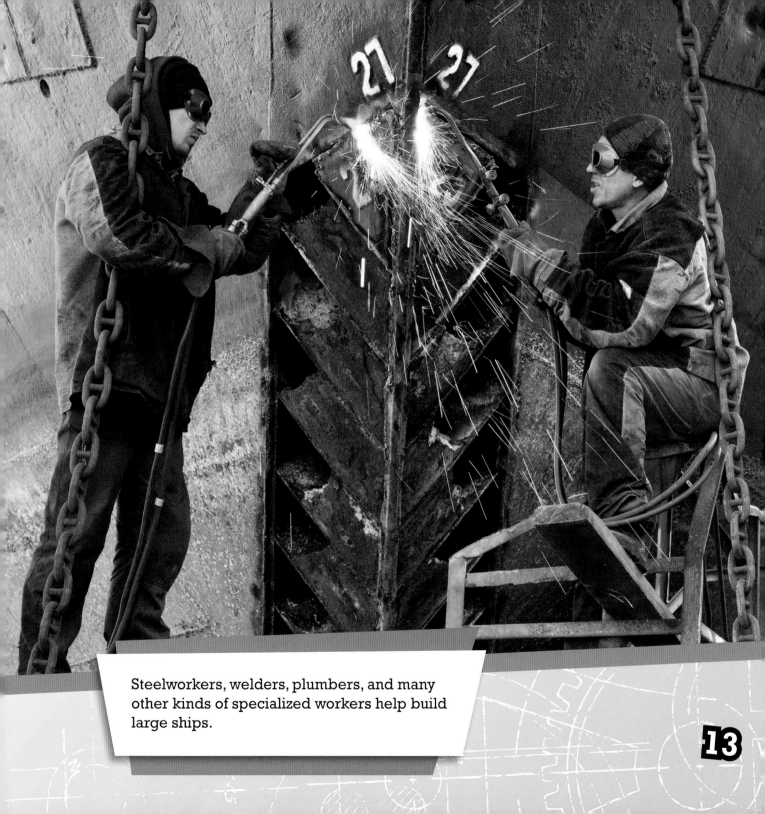

Steelworkers, welders, plumbers, and many other kinds of specialized workers help build large ships.

Taking on Water

Once the hull is built and watertight, the incomplete ship is usually launched, or moved into water. Some small ships are launched sideways, but large ships are launched from the bow (front) to the stern (back) of the boat. Cables, ropes, or chains help keep the hull steady as it's carefully moved on ways into the water to test the ship's buoyancy.

Dry dock–built ships have their docks flooded, which tests for leaks in the hull. Once the hull is complete and the ship floats, construction moves inside.

Building Blocks

Shipbuilders often make a lines plan, a small-scale drawing of a ship, to help design it before construction begins.

Boats under construction aren't put right into open waters, but into closed waterways so they can't be lost easily.

15

Outfitting

The next step in shipbuilding is called outfitting. The ship's engines are fitted, and its steering **equipment** is added. Pipes for plumbing, insulation, and ropes and chains called riggings are put in place. Deck coverings are built to protect the lower levels of the ship.

Ships are often built in sections to make the construction process easier. When a ship is almost complete, it's cleaned, painted, and docked to get ready for the final step in its construction.

Building Blocks

Just like homes, rooms where passengers and crew will stay need beds and bathrooms so everyone feels comfortable while on board.

Every ship has different sections. Some are used for storing fuel, while others are used by passengers for sleeping and eating.

Taking the Test

Naval architects must put their ships through important tests—called trials—to make sure they're **seaworthy**. Ships are tested for their weight and stability. Shipbuilders also find the ship's center of gravity, to better balance the **vessel**.

Ships also go through speed trials, slowly increasing the work the engines and hull have to do in open water. Different tests are done with cargo ships than with cruise ships, but each vessel must be declared safe before starting its life on the water.

Building Blocks

Cargo-ship tanks made for holding liquids are often filled with seawater during trials instead of the liquids they'll carry while in service.

An aircraft carrier must also have its weapons tested as well as its landing pad for planes and helicopters before moving into service.

Make Your Own Boat

Now that you know how ships and boats are built, it's time to make your own. Here's what you need to make your own boat!

What You Need:

- crayon
- paper
- scissors
- straw
- tape

How to:

1. trace the outline of the hull and sail on paper

2. cut out using scissors

3. fold the hull into shape following the dotted lines

4. tape hull together

5. use tape to make boat watertight

6. attach sail to straw

7. tape sail to hull

8. set sail with your new boat!

Glossary

dense: lots of matter packed close together in a small area

design: to create the pattern or shape of something

dry dock: a dock without water used for the building or fixing of ships

equipment: tools and other items needed for a job

fluid: matter that flows and takes the shape of the object holding it

material: matter from which something else can be made

pressure: a force that pushes on something

seaworthy: fit or safe for a sea voyage

stable: steady; not easily tipped over

structure: something built in an arranged way

technology: the way people do something using tools and the tools they use

vessel: any craft bigger than a rowboat and used in water

weld: to join two pieces of metal by heating and pressing them together

For More Information

Books

Abramson, Andra Serlin. *Ships Up Close*. New York, NY: Sterling Publishing, 2008.

Carr, Aaron. *Cruise Ships*. New York, NY: AV2 by Weigl, 2016.

Smith, Ryan A. *Ships: From Start to Finish*. Detroit, MI: Blackbirch Press, 2005.

Websites

Charlestown Navy Yard
nps.gov/bost/learn/historyculture/cny.htm
Learn more about how ships were once built at the Charlestown Navy Yard in Boston.

How to Construct a Simple Boat
instructables.com/id/How-to-Construct-a-Simple-Boat
Find out how to make a simple full-size boat on this site.

Index